The Hunt for Ned October Illustrated

by

Bobby Legend

The Hunt for Ned October (Illustrated)
Published through Legend Publishing Co.

This is a work of fiction. Names, characters, places, and incidents are the product of the author's imagination or are used fictitiously. Any resemblance to actual persons, living or dead, events, or locales is entirely coincidental.

All rights reserved
Copyright © 2006 by Bobby Legend
Illustrations by Virginia Shuman

Interior Book Design and Layout by
www.integrativeink.com

ISBN 978-0615-22553-1

No part of this publication may be reproduced, stored in a retrieval system, or transmitted in any form or by any means electronic, mechanical, photocopying, recording, or otherwise, without the written permission of the author or publisher.

Billy left his friends one day
And moved to a home far, far away

Now Billy lives in a small, three-room home
And sits in his bedroom all alone

Now Billy's depressed and very sad
His mother wanted to make him glad

They both went shopping to change his day
"I wanted to make him happy," his mother would say

But before Billy and his mother entered Boyagian's store
   A crowd of police exited through the front door

The police had arrested two Russian spies
To find out the truth from all of their lies

But Billy and his mother were unaware of the spies
And what they had done and entered Boyagian's store
To shop and have fun

You can buy a costume for Halloween
Whatever you want, I won't intervene

But Billy didn't want a costume that day
He wanted something different, he would say

So he decided to get something wet
And bought a little green turtle for a pet

Now Billy was happy, with a smile on his face
As he carried his pet turtle in a small cardboard case

When he got home, he went right to his room
Then cleared a spot with a small broom

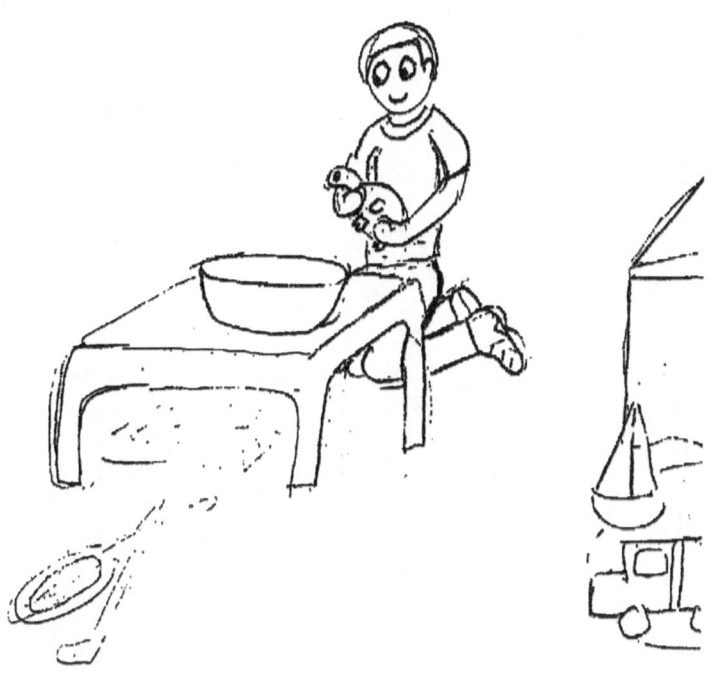

He placed his pet into its bowl near his bed
Then decided to call his pet turtle, Ned

Billy was so happy about his new friend
Oh, how he loved his pet turtle, Ned

But during a tussle with a neighborhood friend
They knocked over a table near Billy's bed

Ned was on that table, in his little bowl
And when he hit the floor, it took its toll

Ned hit the floor on the back of his shell
And blacked out when he fell

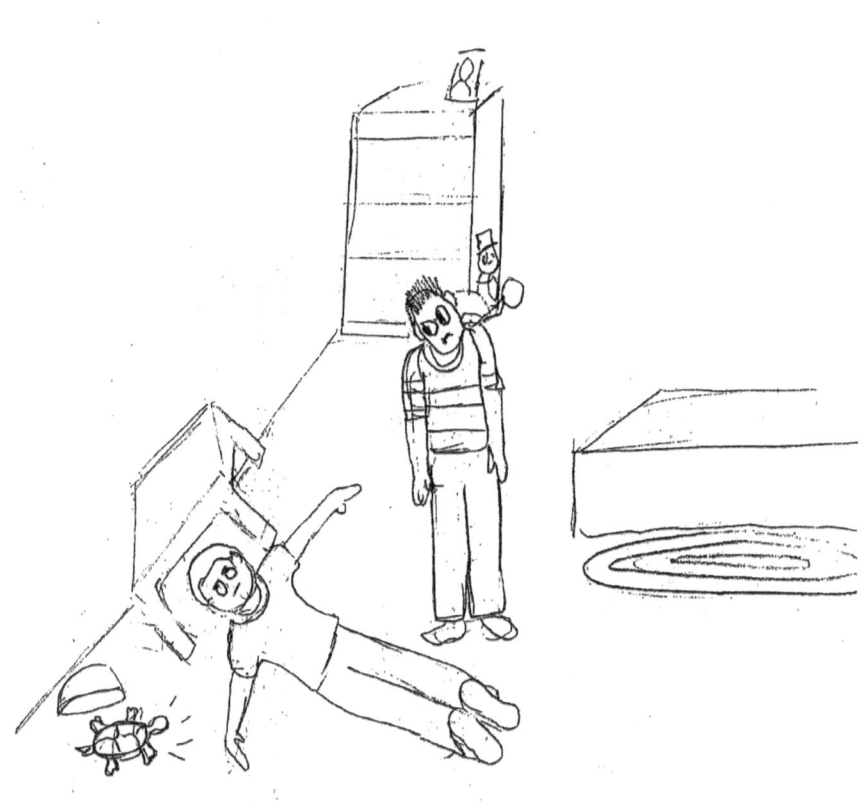

Due to the fight with his neighborhood friend
Both Billy and Ned were hit in the head

When Ned retreated into his shell
Billy was worried and gave a loud yell

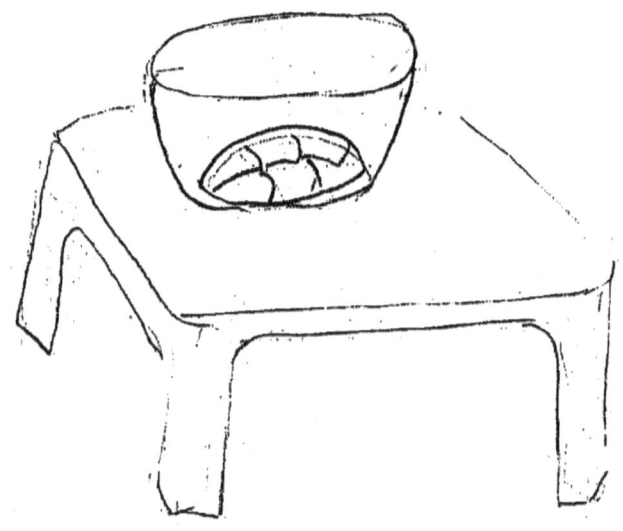

For Ned to come out to talk and play
But Ned was too sick for many a day

Both Billy and Ned became deathly ill
Nothing would help not even a pill

When Billy's illness gets much worse
He's rushed to the hospital before his head bursts

While Billy lay sick and on his death bed
He called for his buddy, his pet turtle, Ned

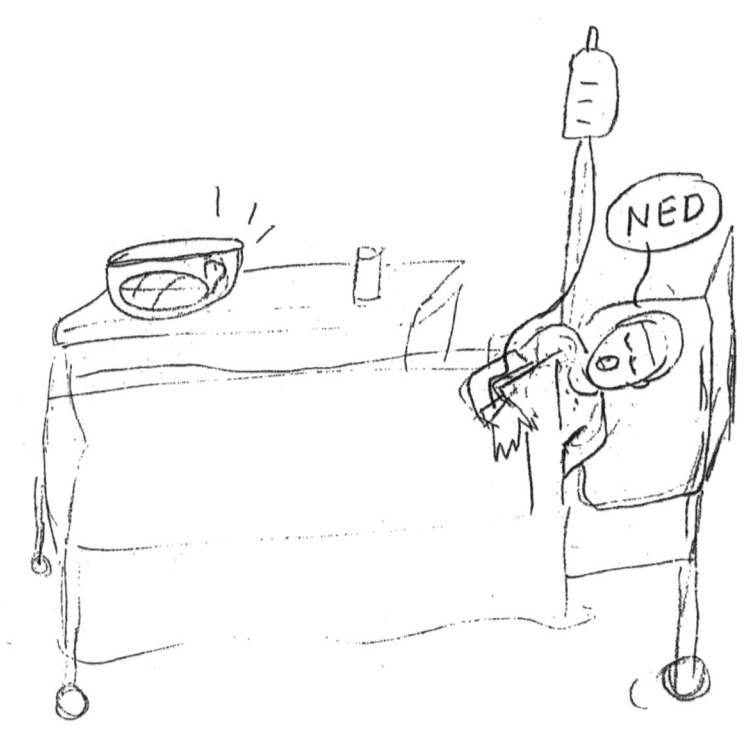

Ned must have heard Billy's yell
Because he awoke and came out of his shell

But suddenly Billy turned for the worse
When his injured head nearly burst

Now Billy lay comatose, almost dead
His mother tried one more thing, his pet turtle, Ned

She placed little Ned on Billy's chest
Hoping to wake him out of his peaceful rest

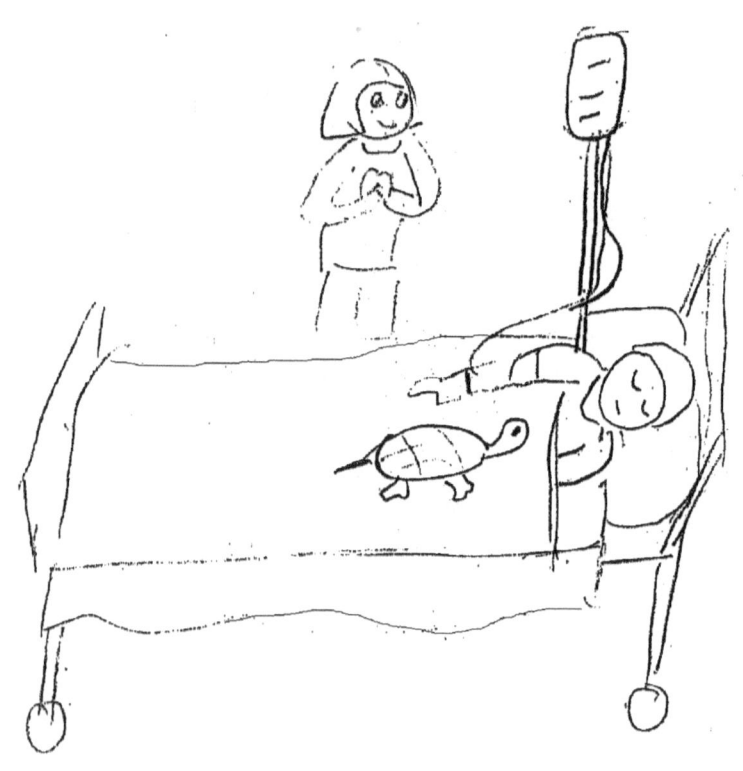

When Ned began to crawl on Billy
His mother wondered if it was silly

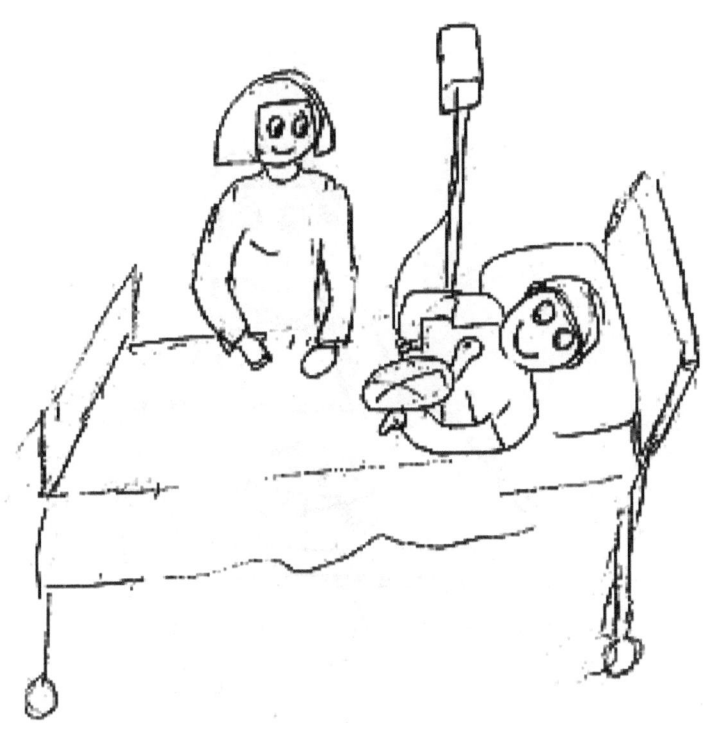

Billy must have felt his pet turtle, Ned
Cause he quickly awoke from the dead

Now Billy's at home thanks to Ned
Now the two are best of friends

But then one day, while cleaning out Ned's bowl
The poor little turtle went down a watery hole

Ned was flushed into a dark, watery grave
But somehow lived and was very brave

Ned fought for his life in the sewers below
Nearly fought to his death with a deadly foe

Ned escaped with his life and was out of breath
But continued on his journey with no fear of death

Billy was busy putting up flyers in town
And hoped his pet turtle would be found

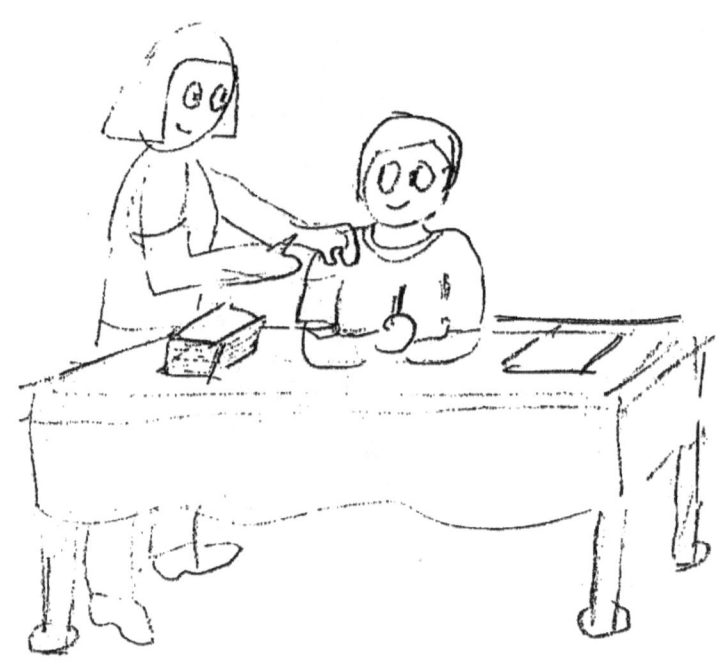

Never give up hope, Billy's mother would shout
Then Billy would smile instead of pout

Billy hoped and prayed everyday
Hoping his pet turtle would find his way

Billy wanted his pet back in his warm little bed
Oh how he loved his pet turtle, Ned

But two Russian spies got involved in the game
Wanting to find fortune and fame

The two Russian spies got into the mix
When they injected a turtle with a precious micro chip

But the cops intervened and the spies were arrested
To have their stories and intelligence tested

But the cops had to let the Russians go
Lack of evidence, don't you know

When the spies were released and got off scot free
They had to find that chip before they could flee

So the spies went looking for their precious chip
That they had injected into one of those turtle's hips

But a hundred of Boyagian's turtles the spies would check
With a miniature fluoroscope, which was a pain in the neck

They had no luck finding the micro chip
That they had injected into a turtle's hip

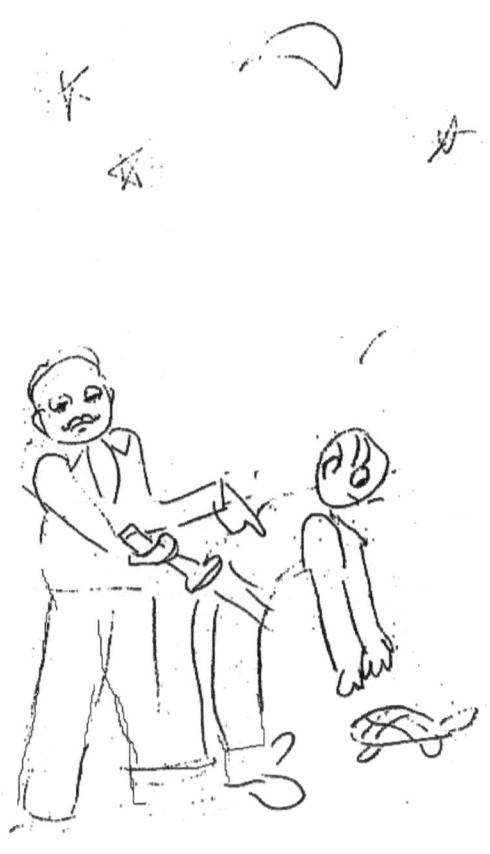

But the spies continued on their quest
Searching and looking, they refused to rest

While the two spies searched high and low
Billy and Ned were always on the go

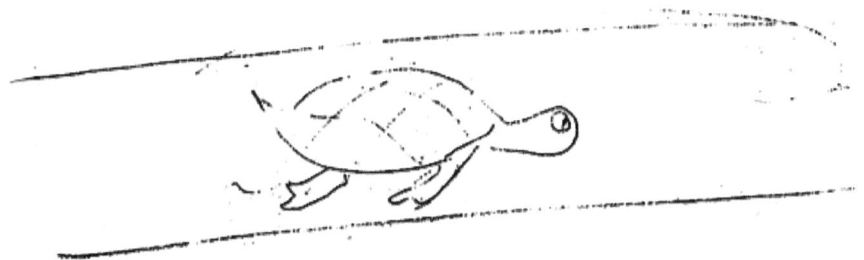

But weeks would pass and hopes would dim
For Ned to find his way home was very slim

But Billy listened to what his mother said
And continued to pray for the safe return of Ned

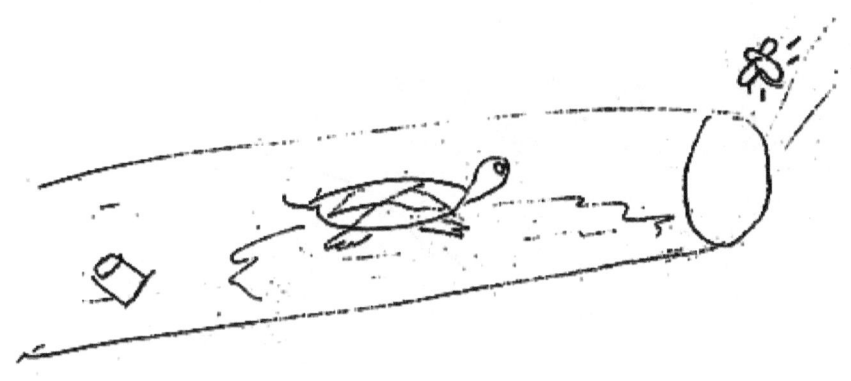

Finally, Ned had made progress and saw some daylight
Then fell into a pool that zapped his strength and might

But Ned was saved by a hippie bee
Brought him to land to set him free

Ned appreciated the help that he got
And Bobby Bee liked Ned a lot

That Bobby took Ned to his little campsite
To meet seven good-hearted insects that weren't too bright

But they soon became friends forever
And helped Ned in his endeavor

Ned crawled over land and many a road
Trying to find his owner's abode

But Ned would never give up
Or Billy might get himself a pup

But as time was short and winter grew near
Freezing to death was Ned's only fear

Then one day, Billy came by
But too far away for Ned to say, hi

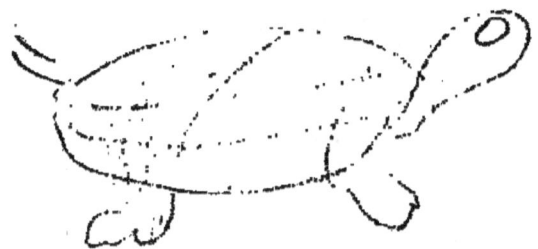

So Ned continued on his quest
Promising, never to rest

Eight little insects ready to fight
To help their friend Ned, with all their might

To get through the obstacles that lay in his way
And get Ned home, in just one short day

But trouble's lurking all around
Even while Billy's putting up flyers in town

The two Russian spies were looking for Ned
They didn't care if he was alive or dead

They did their best to find their chip
That they had injected into a turtle's hip

They looked and looked and had no luck
Then hit poor Billy with their truck

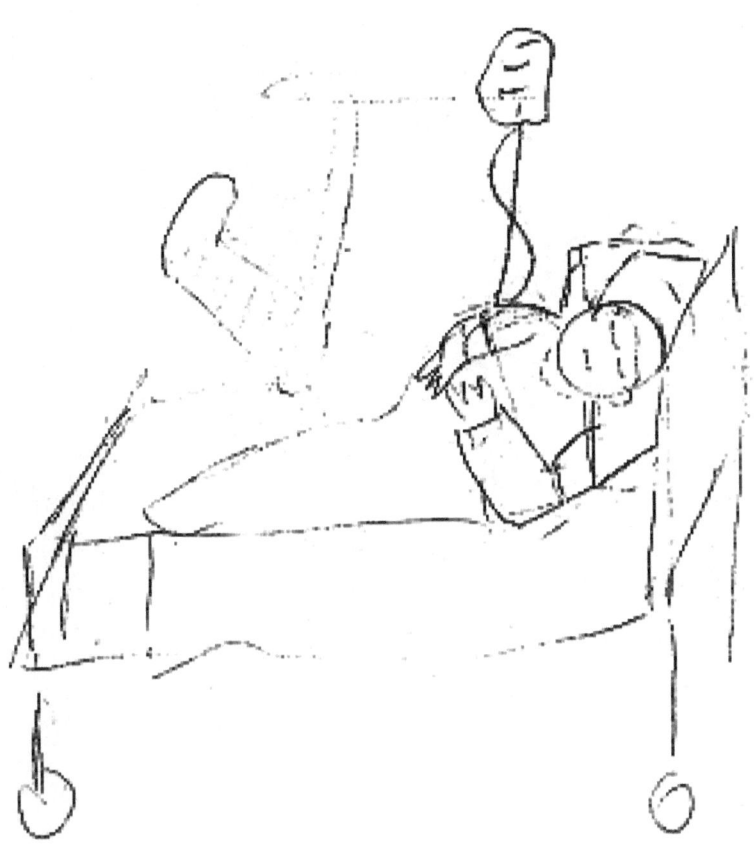

Billy was in traction in a hospital bed
When one of his friends found poor little Ned

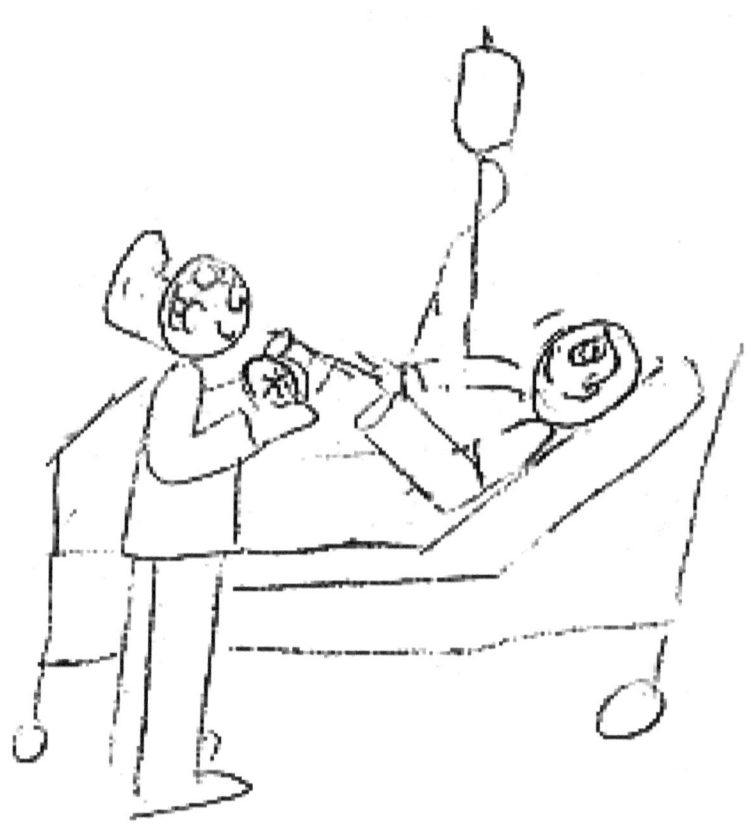

And brought the turtle to Billy's hospital bed
Then Billy saw his pet turtle, Ned

Ned cried for Billy and Billy for Ned
Billy always believed Ned wasn't dead

Billy and his turtle were in the hospital bed
When the two spies burst in to steal Ned

But the cops intervened and stopped their flight
Then deported the two without a fight

Now the two spies are in a Russian jail
Hoping one day that they will get bail

After a while, Billy carried Ned home
Then sat down and wrote this poem

Now Billy and Ned were happy again
But best of all, they're the best of friends

The moral to this story is never give up hope
Keep going forward don't just sit and mope

Keep plugging away at whatever you do
And good things will happen to you